Western Stars

 Country Music Library

Western Stars

of Country Music

ROBERT K. KRISHEF AND BONNIE LAKE

Lerner Publications Company ▪ Minneapolis

ACKNOWLEDGMENTS: The illustrations are reproduced through the courtesy of: pp. 6, 38, Art Rush, Inc.; pp. 12, 24, 27, 30, 35, 42, 66, Country Music Foundation Library and Media Center; pp. 15, 21, Bob Pinson; pp. 16, 18, 22, John Edwards Memorial Foundation; pp. 46, 51, 57, 58, Janice Smith; p. 54, Patsy Montana; p. 60, The Jim Halsey Company, Inc.; p. 71, Board of Directors of the Country Music Association, Inc.

Front cover photo: Patsy Montana

LIBRARY OF CONGRESS CATALOGING IN PUBLICATION DATA

Lake, Bonnie.
    Western stars of country music.

    (Country Music Library)
    Includes index.
    SUMMARY: Presents biographies of western performers in the field of country music: Harry McClintock, Goebel Reeves, Tex Ritter, Gene Autry, Roy Rogers and Dale Evans, Bob Wills, Patsy Montana, Hank Thompson, and Judy Lynn.

    1. Country musicians — The West — Biography — Juvenile literature. [1. Musicians. 2. Country music] I. Krishef, Robert K., joint author. II. Title.

ML3930.A2L33   784'.092'2 [B] [920]   77-90149
ISBN 0-8225-1407-9

Manufactured in the United States of America. Published simultaneously in Canada by J. M. Dent & Sons (Canada) Ltd., Don Mills, Ontario.

International Standard Book Number: 0-8225-1407-9
Library of Congress Catalog Card Number: 77-90149

1 2 3 4 5 6 7 8 9 10 85 84 83 82 81 80 79 78

Contents

Roy Rogers and his famous Palomino, Trigger

Introduction

Country music is a truly American art form. It reflects the character of the land and the people who live in it, perhaps better than any other part of our culture. Like America itself, country music began with the early English, Scotch, and Irish settlers, who brought their fiddles and their music with them to the new land. In song, they told stories of their heritage. These songs were passed from generation to generation, and they gradually came to describe life in America.

That life was often hard, especially in the isolated rural communities of the South and the Southeast. Country music was most popular in those areas. It was a means of expression for hard-working people who battled poverty, illness, exhaustion, and loneliness. They gave vent to their emotions by talking about their troubles in song.

At occasional parties and dances, their spirits were lifted by music that was joyful and animated. Musicians played merrily into the early hours of the morning, while friends and neighbors laughed, clapped, sang, drank, and temporarily forgot about the daily struggle for survival.

The rich music of black Americans—the field hollers, spirituals, and work songs—were also expressions of emotion that became part of the country sound. In addition, blacks taught white musicians exciting, new ways to play the guitar, and that rhythmic, versatile instrument gradually replaced the fiddle as the dominant country music instrument.

Most of this early development of country music took place in the eastern United States. But as people began to move west, country music moved with them. The elements that had made country music popular with the original American settlers also made it popular out West. Traditionally, the music was for independent folk whose roots were in the land or in small, outlying communities. Like the original settlers, the builders of the West were pioneers who faced isolation and loneliness. Western ranchers and cowboys were people of the soil just as much as the farmers who chopped cotton in the fields of the South or who carved a living from rocky New England farm land.

Originally, cowboys sang traditional Irish and

English tunes without accompaniment as they went about their work. Often they kept the old melodies but changed the lyrics to fit their new surroundings. For example, the traditional cowboy refrain "Oh, bury me not on the lone prairie" was adapted from an earlier sentimental ballad that began "O, bury me not in the deep, deep sea." (This ballad was probably derived from songs brought by the original colonists across the Atlantic Ocean.)

The nature of the cowboy's work, however, as well as the character of the land, soon brought about changes in the music that developed in the West. Working with cattle inspired different shouts and sounds than did field work back East. The "coma ti ya youpa ya" of the song "The Chisholm Trail" or the "whoopee ti yi yo" of "Git Along, Little Dogies" would have been out of place behind a plow. But it was in perfect harmony with the clatter of horses' hoofs or the cowboys' exuberant efforts to get a cattle herd moving.

Some of the music developed in the West reflected sounds that the cowboys learned from others. Swiss groups who toured the area in the 1880s taught cowboys how to yodel. From south of the border came the "hot" rhythms of Mexico, which were combined with cowboy music to become what is sometimes referred to as "Tex-Mex" music. These factors, plus the feeling of freedom in the West, helped to create a receptive atmosphere for the lusty, spirited music played at ranch dances. Eventually, this music evolved into the rhythmic dance music called *western swing.*

As the West grew, it increasingly captured the attention and imagination of people all over the country. The Southwest and West were dramatized first in popular literature and subsequently through silent films, over radio, and through sound movies (the "talkies") beginning in the late 1920s. There came to be a romantic aura about the rugged individualism of the frontier, with its cowboys, drifters, and gunfighters. Early in the 1900s, a favorite theme for song lyrics was that of the drifter—either cowboy or hobo—who was lonely, yet lonely by choice and happy to be free. The cowboy became a popular figure in films, and in the 1930s, singing western movies became a national phenomenon. Cowboys like Gene Autry who starred in these films became American folk heroes.

The cowboy's popularity made the western style of dress fashionable, and it was adopted by many country entertainers who had never even sat on a horse. The "western look"—gaudy, sequined versions of the cowboy suit with matching hat and boots—is still a favorite among many entertainers today.

Western music, the "child" of country music, has grown up to become important in its own right. And it has had a tremendous influence on country music in general. Perhaps the most telling reminder of the influence of the West lies in the term "country and western" music. For years, this term was often used to describe all country music, although western music was really just one branch, or type, of country. Now the industry has more or less dropped the term. (For instance, the Academy of Country and Western Music, founded in 1965, has since shortened its name to the more general Academy of Country Music.) But dropping the term has not changed history. A discussion of the evolution of country music, and of its stars, would not be complete without mention of performers with western roots. The West is alive today in country music, and country music is more alive because of its western heritage. The contributions of many great artists made this happen. This book is about some of those artists.

Harry McClintock   1

In his song "Big Rock Candy Mountain," Harry McClintock sang about a hobo hiking down the railroad track, saying, "Boys, I'm not turning, I'm headed for a land that's far away." The hobo and the cowboy—both lonely wanderers who rejected the idea of settling permanently, of having "roots" or family—were two of the most common figures in country music during the 1920s and 1930s. In those hard times, the idea of the drifter's life had considerable appeal for many people who yearned to escape from the drudgery to which they were tied.

Some performers have managed to sing convincingly about drifting without ever having done it. But Harry ("Haywire Mac") McClintock learned first-hand about life on the road. One of the first singers to record cowboy and hobo songs, Mac was born in Knoxville, Tennessee, on October 8, 1882.

His early musical training was chiefly as a choir-
boy in the Episcopal church. This helped to
develop his voice. But he developed his singing
style and his knowledge and feeling for western
songs after leaving home.

Mac was only 14 years old when he ran away
from home to join a dog and pony show. When the
show's season ended, he found his way to New
Orleans. There he worked on an old riverboat for
a while in exchange for food and a bunk. But it
wasn't long before he found a new way to make a
living. In the New Orleans waterfront saloons,
young Mac soon learned that he could make a few
dollars by singing for the patrons. This was a dis-
covery that changed his life. He saw that as long
as he could entertain people, he would never have
to worry about going hungry.

By the time Mac turned 16, the United States
had entered the Spanish-American War. The boy's
life took another fateful turn when he hitched a
ride on a troop train bound for an Army camp in
Tennessee. It was in Tennessee that Mac first met
the Army teamsters and packers. In those days,
the Army used teams of horses and wagons, as well
as trains, to transport supplies and ammunition.
The men who packed the wagons and handled
the teams were civilians hired by the Army. They
were rugged men from the West who could handle
horses and could live under the hardest condi-

tions. Young Mac admired them and hung around them, learning their trade. At the same time, he learned many of the western songs that the workers sang.

In 1898 Mac was hired by the Army and shipped to the Philippines, where he spent two tough years as a packer. Later he was sent to China with the Allied Relief Expedition.

In the Army, Mac often entertained his fellow soldiers with cowboy songs and tales of the open

Mac McClintock (standing, far right)
with his band, "Mac's Haywire Orchestry"

This sheet music, published in 1932, featured some of Mac's most popular hits.

road. During this period, he began to write and sing songs about the common man. For one of the songs he wrote, "Hallelujah, I'm A Bum," he borrowed the melody from an old English hymn, "Revive Us Again." He added new lyrics that described the life of the out-of-work drifter. In 1908, the song became an unofficial theme for the Industrial Workers of the World (IWW) labor movement.

After his stint in the Army ended, Mac spent many years drifting and singing in mining camps and saloons all over the country. Finally, in 1925, he got a break. He was offered his own radio show over KFRC in San Francisco. The show, which featured cowboy songs, surprised everyone by being highly successful. At the peak of his singing career, Mac was also recording for Victor Records. His were the first recordings ever made of such songs as "Red River Valley," "When The Work's All Done This Fall," "Cowboy's Lament," and "Bury Me Not On The Lone Prairie."

For five or six years, Mac enjoyed great success as a singer of cowboy and hobo songs. But his career declined in the 1930s. The depression had hit the country, and relatively few records were being sold. In addition, the age of the singing western movie was beginning. Mac was an authentic drifter, but he was in his 50s and didn't fit the Hollywood image of a movie hero. Still, Mac McClintock had had an important role in the evolution of western music. Like the pioneer settlers who first cleared the land, Mac's early recordings helped to clear the way and create the climate of acceptance for the superstar cowboys who came after him.

Goebel Reeves 2

When Goebel Reeves was a young boy in the early 1900s, he met a hobo. Hobos were drifters—men without homes or families—who rode around the country in railroad freight cars, scrounging for food and shelter wherever they could get them. Usually called "bums," hobos were frowned upon by "respectable" people.

Young Goebel, however, felt sorry for this hobo. It was cold, and the boy gave the ragged man his brand new overcoat. Goebel's parents spanked him when they found out. But they couldn't stop what was the beginning of a fascination with the hobo way of life.

The life of a lonely drifter, "riding the rails," must have seemed romantic and adventurous to young Goebel. Born on October 9, 1899, in Sherman, Texas, he had a comfortable if unexciting childhood. His mother taught voice and piano.

His father was a shoe salesman and later a member of the Texas legislature. When Goebel was in his teens, he worked for the legislature as a page, running errands and performing other tasks. But during that time he continued to dream of drifting, and he kept on learning songs about life on the open road.

By the time Goebel was 18, World War I was raging in Europe. So he enlisted in the Army and was sent to France, where he was wounded at the front lines. After being discharged, he returned home. But he was restless and felt the urge to drift. He soon began his travels, working at whatever jobs he could find, sometimes paying for meals by singing a few songs and playing his guitar.

From his experiences of cold, lonely nights, clattering freight cars, tough railroad cops, and "jungles" where hobos gathered, Goebel developed his down-to-earth song lyrics and style of singing. His style included yodeling. Later, he would state that he had taught one of the most famous country singers of all time, Jimmie Rodgers, how to yodel.

Rodgers, Vernon Dalhart, and other singers began to make records in the middle 1920s. Seeing how successful they were becoming, Goebel went to New York to try his luck. He recorded under several different names, including nicknames like the Yodeling Rustler, the Yodeling Wrangler, and the Broadway Rustler. Ultimately he became known, appropriately enough, as the Texas Drifter.

For the next 15 years, Goebel wrote and recorded hobo and cowboy songs for Brunswick Records, the McGregor Company in Hollywood, California, and other companies. His big break came in 1931, when he was discovered by producer Graham McNamee of the National Broadcasting Company (NBC). McNamee heard Goebel singing and yodeling, and signed him to appear on a radio

Goebel Reeves sang and strummed his guitar as a guest on numerous radio shows.

show hosted by Rudy Vallee, a leading singer of popular music. Goebel received $350 for his appearance. He admitted later that, when he had signed the contract, he had thought the "three-fifty" meant three dollars and fifty cents!

Goebel won many fans with his records, his radio guest spots, and his appearances on the vaudeville circuit. Still, he did not have a steady or consistent career. Country people liked him, but city people thought he was too unsophisticated.

The colorful character who sang about the wandering life of the hobo and the cowboy was himself an authentic drifter.

Another complication was his wanderlust—his desire to travel. He rarely stayed in one place for more than a few months. Often his friends and even his own family had trouble keeping track of him. Once he even wound up in Japan!

Although Goebel never attained the fame of Jimmie Rodgers, he did introduce songs that added to the folklore surrounding the figure of the drifter. Some of the songs he recorded include "The Cowboy's Prayer," "The Hobo and The Cop," "The Texas Drifter's Warning," "I'm Just A Lonesome Cowboy," and "Bar None Ranch." One song that Goebel wrote, "I've Ranged, I've Roamed, I've Traveled," was recorded and made famous by Jimmie Rodgers.

The Texas Drifter died in 1959. He was living quietly at the time, out of public view, in a suburb of Los Angeles. Most fans had long forgotten him. Yet Goebel Reeves's fascination with the cowboy and the hobo way of life had left an unmistakable imprint upon country music, and his influence is still felt today.

Tex Ritter 3

If Woodward Maurice (Tex) Ritter had followed his parents' advice, he might have become a famous attorney rather than a famous western star. The boy had a sharp mind. He excelled in debating, and was top student in his high school class in 1922. Young Tex was deeply interested in the legal profession. For as long as he could remember, he had loved to read about and listen to lawyers. History was another of his favorite subjects; even as a high school student, he was considered an expert on the history of the Southwest. After high school, Tex went on to study law at both the University of Texas and Northwestern University. But even then he felt torn between taking his parents' advice and becoming an attorney, or becoming a singer. For this native of east Texas had roots in music that were deep and heartfelt.

Born on January 12, 1906, Tex had grown up singing with his family at community sings, in the church choir, and even at horseshoe pitching contests. Later, during his university studies, he "moonlighted" with jobs on the side as a radio singer. Listeners liked his deep baritone voice and sizable repertoire of old cowboy songs. Those songs were his favorites, perhaps because they reminded him of his father, who had once been a cowboy.

Finally, the lure of show business won out. Tex left school, went on tour with a western band, and arrived in New York City in 1930 with $30 in cash and high hopes. Some lean and hungry days followed. But Tex persevered until he got the part of a cowboy in a production called *Green Grow The Lilacs.* This was the Broadway play later revised into the smash hit *Oklahoma!*

Tex made his stage role pay off. He landed a recording contract with Columbia Records and released two hits, "A-Ridin' Old Paint" and "Goodbye Ole Paint." The latter song was one of the oldest in American cowboy folklore. A typically haunting, mournful western song, it told about a cowboy who was "a-leavin' Cheyenne" without his faithful horse. Tex's records sold well, and he also had starring roles in radio shows such as "The Lone Star Rangers," New York's "Barn Dance," "Tex Ritter's Campfires," and a children's program called "Cowboy Tom's Roundup." By 1934, he was well established as a big-time radio performer.

In 1936, Tex made his movie debut in *Song Of The Gringo,* a Grand National Pictures release. Over the next 20 years, he had parts or starred in more than 75 musical Westerns for 5 different studios. He rode the range on his famous horse, White Flash, catching bad guys, rescuing lovely ladies from certain disaster, and pausing every now and then for a song. The plots of his movies were so thin and unimportant that, as he later admitted with a chuckle, he sometimes filmed for

In this film Tex (center) *sings by the campfire while Red Foley accompanies him on the guitar.*

an entire day without having the slightest idea what the movie was about! But the public didn't mind. They came for exciting action and good music. For years Tex was among the 10 best-paid actors in Hollywood.

Tex's reputation as a western singer kept him in the public eye even after cowboy movies began to lose popularity. He had numerous hit records, such as "Jealous Heart," "Hillbilly Heaven" (his biggest), the humorous "Life Gits Teejus, Don't It," "Jingle, Jangle, Jingle," "The San Antone Story," and "The Wayward Wind." One of his most memorable hits was the theme song from the movie *High Noon.* The film, which starred Gary Cooper and Grace Kelly, presented a typically romanticized image of the American West. It was about a heroic sheriff (Cooper) left by the townspeople to face desperate outlaws alone in a shootout at noon. The sheriff won—and so did the picture, which received several awards from the film industry, including one for the theme song sung by Tex.

Throughout his career, Tex was highly respected in show business, not only for his professional accomplishments but for his personal integrity as well. He was admired for his intelligence and gentlemanly manner, and beloved for his generosity. His encouragement and help started many performers, including Buck Owens, Hank Thompson, and Jim Reeves, on their way to success.

At one point, Tex's popularity led him to make a bid for the United States Senate, and then for the governorship of Tennessee. He was defeated, however, in those elections. But in the country music field, Tex was always a winner. He was twice elected president of the Country Music Association. In 1964, he became the first living person to be elected to the Country Music Hall of Fame.

Tex died on January 2, 1974. His plaque at the Country Music Hall of Fame is now a lasting tribute to the memory of the deep voiced Texas singer, who made the country sit up and take notice of the cowboy. The plaque cites Tex as an "...untiring pioneer and champion of the country and western music industry." It further reads: "His devotion to his god, his family, and his country is a continuing inspiration to his countless friends throughout the world."

Gene Autry 4

The bad guys have burned down the hero's ranch house, attacked his best gal, beaten up his mother, and rustled his cattle. "Ah'm gonna get those low-down polecats if it's the last thing I do," drawls the heroic cowpuncher. "First, though, folks, ah'm gonna sing you a little song."

So, more or less, went a standard joke in the 1930s and 1940s about the plots of movies starring cowboy singers. Most of the jokes were about movies made by the "most tuneful cowpuncher" of them all, Gene Autry. For it was Gene who was largely responsible for making popular that special kind of movie called the "singing Western." In the singing Western, the music was as important as the action. The hero was a brave, noble cowpoke who faced all danger alone. He could outride, out-rope, and outfight any *hombre* in the West. But no matter how rough the going got, he always had time to pick up his guitar and sing a song.

The plots of Gene Autry's movies were usually pretty thin and unrealistic. But that didn't bother his fans. They loved the romance, the adventure, and the music. During his career, Gene made more than 100 films for Republic Studios. He was justifiably billed as "America's Number One Singing Cowboy." For seven straight years, his movies sold more tickets than did movies of any other western singing star.

Unlike some movie cowboys, Gene really was from the West. He was born September 29, 1907, on a cattle farm near Tioga, Texas. When he was quite young, his family moved to a ranch in Oklahoma. Gene showed an early interest in music. He often sang in the choir of the Baptist church where his grandfather was the preacher. When he was 11 years old, he bought his first guitar "on time." He put a dollar down and paid 50 cents a week until the guitar was paid for.

Although he dreamed of becoming a professional singer, after high school Gene needed to earn a living. So at the age of 17, he got a job as night telegrapher with the St. Louis & Frisco Railroad. Between sending and receiving messages, he practiced the guitar and developed a crooning, yodeling style of singing in imitation of his idol, Jimmie Rodgers. In his spare time, Gene sang at local clubs to earn extra money. He "passed the hat," asking for contributions from the audience as payment for entertaining. But collections on many occasions totaled less than 50 cents!

Young Gene was inspired to keep on singing, however, by an incident that occurred one night when he was working as a telegrapher. A lanky stranger stopped in to send a telegram, spied the guitar, and asked Gene for a song. Gene obliged with two songs—"They Plowed The Old Trail Under" and "Casey Jones." The stranger was impressed. He told Gene to go on the radio instead of wasting time sending telegrams. When the man had gone, Gene looked at the signature on the message. It was that of Will Rogers, the famous comedian and philosopher.

Hard times hit the railroad soon after Gene got Rogers's advice, and Gene lost his job. But he still had a free railroad pass. So he headed for New York City. There, he walked the streets with his guitar under his arm, knocking on doors. He tried and tried to get an audition. Finally, frustrated by lack of success, he started singing and playing in the waiting room at Victor Recording Studios.

That got him attention—and an audition. The Victor executives liked Gene but felt that he needed more experience. He wasn't hired, but he did leave with a letter of introduction, which he used to get a job at KVOO Radio in Tulsa, Oklahoma. The station billed him as "Oklahoma's Singing Cowboy." There, Gene began to develop his own mellow singing style. With the assistance of a talent scout, Art Satherly, he started to make records. By 1929 Gene was recording for Victor, the very company that had sent him home for more experience only a year before!

Gene did well in Tulsa and as a result caught on with WLS Radio in Chicago. He became a performer on the WLS "National Barn Dance," a popular Saturday night country music program. It was during his time with this program that Gene began to gain national recognition. The Sears Roebuck Company used the young singer in its catalog to promote Gene Autry "Roundup" guitars for $9.95. And there were full-page ads in the catalog for his records. Hundreds of thousands of copies of "My Old Pal Of Yesterday," "A Gangster's Wedding," and his most popular song, "That Silver-Haired Daddy Of Mine," were sold, helping to make Gene's name familiar from coast to coast.

In 1934, Gene left the Barn Dance and went to California. Art Satherly, the talent scout who had helped him before, persuaded Republic Studios to give Gene a small role in a film called *In Old Santa Fe*. The movie starred Ken Maynard, a popular film cowboy who sometimes sang a song or two. Moviegoers noticed Gene instantly in the film, and fan mail soon convinced the studio that it had made a "find." Gene turned out eight more movies in his first year. He soon acquired his movie "sidekick," Smiley Burnette, and his famous Palomino horse, Champion. With this team, Gene proceeded to capture the hearts of the nation's Saturday matinee crowd.

In movies like *Mexicali Rose* and *Tumbling Tumbleweeds,* Gene combined the image of a smart, tough cowboy with that of a warm and sincere country singer. On the screen he sometimes seemed rather shy, or even awkward. But that didn't hurt his popularity. According to one critic, his fans probably liked him all the more for it.

In this publicity shot for the movie Rancho Grande, *Gene poses with Smiley Burnette, June Story, Mary Lee — the "Pals of the Golden West."*

The 1930s were busy years for Gene. In addition to appearing in the movies, he had his own CBS radio show, "Melody Ranch." The show, which began in 1939, was so popular that it ran for 17 years. Gene also toured the country with his Gene Autry Rodeo, which featured trick riding and roping, clowns, and, of course, music. He continued to write and record a great many of his most popular songs, too.

By the late 1930s, Gene was an American institution. He even had a town in Oklahoma named for him. As a young singer with the National Barn Dance, he had once been discouraged enough to scrawl "Gene Autry, America's Biggest Flop" on the door of his dressing room. Now the door was framed under glass in the lobby of the theater. He was even popular abroad. When he visited Ireland in 1939, more than a million people jammed the streets of Dublin to see him.

Then, World War II abruptly interrupted Gene's career. In 1942 he joined the Army Air Corps and became a pilot with the Air Transport Command, flying supply planes in India and Burma. After the war ended in 1945, Gene plunged into a variety of business activities. Seeing the potential of television, he organized a film company, Flying A Pictures, which produced half-hour Gene Autry shows as well as the popular "Range Rider" series. He also made profitable investments in the California Angels baseball team, music publishing houses, hotels, motels, radio stations, and a record company.

In 1969, Gene was elected to the Nashville Country Music Hall of Fame. He was recognized for his singing on the radio, for his stardom as a singing cowboy in films, for selling millions of records, and for writing or co-writing more than 250 songs, ranging from traditional country material such as "Tears On My Pillow" to Christmas favorites such as "Here Comes Santa Claus." In addition, many critics credit Gene with helping to make country music popular and accepted among the general public. The singing Western lent romance and glamor to what many people had once thought of as "hillbilly" music. Along with Jimmie Rodgers, Gene is also given much credit for starting the trend among country singers toward wearing western clothing. Now many country stars wear cowboy hats and western shirts, even though they don't necessarily sing cowboy songs.

Today, Gene is a millionaire businessman and a legend in the country music industry. Still, millions of fans do not think of him in such lofty terms. For them, the name Gene Autry brings back the magic of the Saturday matinee—black hats and bad guys, six-guns that seemed to shoot forever without reloading, and the bashful buckaroo winning the West with a song.

Roy Rogers and Dale Evans 5

Gene Autry, Tex Ritter, and several other cowboy singers have each been considered by their respective supporters to be "king" of the western singing stars. But to most of the fans of shoot-'em-up movies from the 1940s on, smiling, squinty-eyed Roy Rogers was, is, and always will be the only true "King of the Cowboys." That, in fact, was how Republic Pictures billed him, and legitimately so.

Before signing with Republic, Roy had had small film roles as a singing cowboy for Columbia Studios. But in 1937, Republic wanted a backup star to its top actor, Gene Autry. So they put Gene and Roy together in some films. At first, of course, Roy took second billing to Gene. But when Gene left to join the Army Air Corps during World War II, Roy became the studio's number one singing cowboy. He made 86 pictures for Republic, and was "King of the Cowboys" for 12 years. By 1945, only four movie and show business greats — Clark Gable, Bing Crosby, Gary Cooper, and Spencer Tracy — led Roy in the popularity polls. As a cowboy star, Roy had no rivals.

Roy became a cowboy star primarily because he was well prepared for such a role, even though he did not come from the Southwest as did most famous singing cowboys. He was born Leonard Slye on November 5, 1912, in Cincinnati, Ohio — certainly a far cry from the West. But when he was a boy, the family moved to a small farm near Portsmouth, Ohio, the city where his father worked in a shoe factory. On the farm, Roy learned to ride horses. He also learned music at an early age from his mandolin-playing parents. By the time he was a teenager, he was singing and yodeling, and serving as the caller at county square dances.

During the depression of the 1930s, Mary, one of Roy's sisters, was married and went to live in southern California. Seeing that jobs were becoming scarce at the shoe factory in Ohio, Roy's father suddenly decided that the family should take the opportunity to visit Mary. Once in California, he thought they might find jobs, too. So they climbed into a 1923 Dodge flatbed truck and headed West.

Roy and his father worked as migrant fruit pickers in the California peach orchards for a few months before the Slyes decided to return to Ohio. But Roy had fallen in love with the California sun and the ocean, and before long he went back to California to stay.

He tried various jobs—driving a sand and gravel truck, picking beans, and even boxing, at which he earned one dollar for three rounds of fighting. More and more, however, he turned to music, making good use of his clean-cut looks, boyish charm, good guitar playing, and pleasant voice. He played with several groups, including the Rocky Mountaineers and the Texas Outlaws, before becoming lead singer—under the name Dick Weston—with the Pioneer Trio. The trio, which included Bob Nolan and Tim Spencer, was to become famous in the movies and in country music as the Sons of the Pioneers. It was during his three-year period with this group that Roy began to appear in the small cowboy roles that eventually led him to film stardom as Roy Rogers.

Roy's leading lady in most of his films was a blonde singer named Dale Evans. If Roy was the king of the singing Westerns, Dale was certainly the queen, and a successful vocalist in her own right.

She was born Frances Octavia Smith on October 31, 1912, in Uvalde, Texas. Later she moved with her family to Osceola, Arkansas. She married when she was only 16, and after the marriage ended in

Originally a pop singer, Dale Evans began to develop her cowgirl image after starring with Roy Rogers in the movie Swing Your Partner.

divorce two years later, she launched a singing career to support herself and her small son. Starting in the early 1930s on a radio station in Memphis, Tennessee, she moved on to other radio jobs in Louisville, Kentucky, Dallas, Texas, and finally Chicago, Illinois.

Although she was originally from Texas, Dale didn't sing country songs. In Chicago, she sang popular songs on the radio and on the stage with Anson Weeks's band, a well-known group of that time. She impressed audiences enough to earn an engagement at the Chez Paree, one of the most exclusive night clubs in the country. That led to appearances on the popular "Charlie McCarthy and Edgar Bergen" network radio show, and ultimately to a movie contract. In 1943, Dale was cast as a cowgirl in *Swing Your Partner.* Her leading man was, of course, Roy Rogers. It was the beginning of a partnership that was to last for nearly 20 years on film. In actual life, Roy and Dale were married in 1947, about a year after the death of Roy's first wife. Today, 30 years later, they are still happily married.

From the beginning, the Rogers-Evans partnership on the screen and off has been a model of traditional values. Roy and Dale always wanted their movies to be wholesome entertainment for all ages, and particularly for the children who went to the Saturday matinees. In their films, the plots were always the same. The good guys in the white hats *always* won, and they won without unusual violence. Roy never "killed" anyone in his pictures.

The supporting cast of their films became almost as beloved as the two stars. Roy had his ever-present sidekick, played by either Pat Brady or Gabby Hayes. And, of course, there was Bullet, the faithful dog. Dale rode a horse called Buttermilk. Roy's horse was the famous Palomino, Trigger, who had so much "horse sense" that it almost seemed as if he could round up the bad guys all by himself!

When the popularity of Western movies began to decline, Dale and Roy eased gracefully into their own radio show, and then into television. During the 1950s, they made 104 half-hour TV films, and 90 one-hour features, which are still being seen in some cities. Their theme song, "Happy Trails," became closely identified with them, and Roy had numerous hit records through the years, including "Skip To My Lou," "You Can't Break My Heart," "Home On The Range," "Old Fashioned Cowboy," and "My Chicashay Gal." Roy has continued to record successfully: he had a hit single record, "Hoppy, Gene, and Me," in 1974, and another, "Cowboy Heaven," in 1975. "Cowboy Heaven" was part of a new album called *Happy Trails To You.* He and Dale have also made many successful recordings together. Some of these have been religious songs written by Dale.

Both Dale and Roy remain active in various endeavors today. They own race horses, real estate, and restaurants; there are almost 200 Roy Rogers Restaurants throughout the country. The couple also operates the Roy Rogers museum about a mile from their desert home in Apple Valley, California. They are in demand at rodeos and state fairs, and they still set attendance records with their appearances at places such as Madison Square Garden and the Houston Astrodome.

Dale has even had success as an author. In 1975 her Bicentennial book, *Let Freedom Ring,* was well received. It was her 14th book to date. Most of her books deal with inspirational or patriotic themes. Her first book, *Angel Unaware,* was a true story about the death of the Rogers' two-year-old mongoloid daughter. Of the nine children that were either born to or adopted by Dale and Roy, two others have also died.

Dale and Roy have had to deal with very real tragedy in their lives. But they are not embittered over past grief. They prefer to look ahead and have maintained their faith in life and in God. They devote themselves extensively to charitable causes—especially those dedicated to orphaned or disabled children. The Rogers have received numerous awards for their charitable work from the American Legion, American Red Cross, National Association for Retarded Children, Muscular Dystrophy Association, and many religious groups.

Their stories were once told by Ralph Edwards on the television program "This Is Your Life." Edwards said afterward that he had had more requests to repeat the film of that show than any he had ever done. The show was repeated three times.

Obviously their fans are not about to forget Roy Rogers and Dale Evans. The couple's long and successful trail through life has brought happiness to many people, and has left no doubt about who are the reigning king and queen of western country.

Bob Wills 6

Long before Bob Wills was born on March 6, 1905,
fiddlers in the Old West were playing "western
swing"—a high-spirited kind of music popular at
ranch dances and house parties. Bob Wills didn't
invent western swing but, more than any other
person, he was responsible for modernizing the
rhythmic, danceable sound and popularizing it
throughout the country. Known for good reason as
the "King of Western Swing," he sold more than
20 million records during a career that spanned
over 40 years.

Like so many country musicians, Bob came from
humble surroundings. He was one of 10 children
born to Emma and John Wills, poor tenant farmers
from Limestone County, Texas. His given name
was James Robert. But he was called "Jim" by his
father, "Robby" by his mother, "Jim Rob" by his
brothers and sisters, and eventually "Bob" by the
public.

Bob's mother had once been the champion girl cotton picker of her county. When Bob was a boy, she needed all her skill. For the Wills family raised small crops of cotton and corn—sometimes not enough of either—on their farm. Bob's father, John, often played the fiddle at dances to help make mortgage payments. Like his own father before him, John was an excellent fiddler.

Young Bob grew up surrounded by the exciting music of the Southwest. Many of his aunts, uncles, and cousins were musically inclined. In addition, he had many black childhood friends with whom he played and later worked side-by-side in the cotton fields. From them, he learned the haunting rhythms of jazz and blues. One day he would combine these sounds with others—New Orleans jazz, old-time Texas fiddle music, and Mexican music—to create a new form of western swing.

By the time he was 11, Bob was playing guitar, mandolin, and fiddle with his father at dances. His natural talent for playing the fiddle, especially, was obvious. Within a few years he was heard on local radio stations. But it was still a long time before Bob took music seriously as a career. Before that happened, he would leave home periodically— the first time when he was just 16—to work at many different jobs. At the age of 23, the tough, stocky young man had already been a preacher, barber, cotton picker, hobo, carpenter, zinc worker, roughneck (a worker on an oil-drilling rig), telephone line surveyor, shoe shiner, insurance man, rooming house manager, and automobile salesman, as well as a part-time fiddler.

In 1929, Bob moved to Fort Worth, Texas, where he decided to start a band. The "band" consisted of himself on the fiddle and Herman Arnspiger on guitar. Called the Wills Fiddle Band, the duo played at dances and even made a couple of records. When they added a vocalist, Milton Brown, and two more musicians in 1930, they changed their name to Aladdin's Laddies.

Aladdin's Laddies were good, but the times were not. It was during the depression, and work was hard to get. Bob, however, had an idea. What if he used his musical ability to gain an affiliation with a large company? Perhaps he could get the company to sponsor a show featuring his music. Then he would have both steady employment *and* the chance to perform. The idea worked. Bob and his band got a radio show sponsored by the Burrus Mill and Elevator Company of Fort Worth, a milling company that made Light Crust flour. So Aladdin's Laddies became the Light Crust Doughboys. The Doughboys' show was to be the turning point of Bob's career.

At 7:00 each morning, the Doughboys played over KFJZ radio in Fort Worth. During the day, they worked for their sponsor as truck drivers or salesmen, or in other capacities. At night, they made personal appearances for their sponsor. They were a hit, and their show was picked up by the Southwest Quality Network. It was broadcast at 12:30 noon in Oklahoma City, Fort Worth, and in other towns all over the Southwest. Many a tired farmer spent his lunch break listening to Bob Wills's Doughboys while waiting for his biscuits and black-eyed peas.

Eventually Bob added more members to his band. He and some of the Doughboys made their first records, for Victor, in 1932. But the association with Burrus Mill and Elevator Company started to go downhill. There were disputes with the company's president, W. Lee O'Daniel, who wanted the Doughboys to stop making personal appearances at dances. There were also arguments about salaries, Bob's right to hire and fire musicians, missed broadcasts, and other matters.

Finally, the Doughboys disbanded. Members scattered in various directions, finding jobs with different groups. But most of them eventually rejoined Bob when he picked up his career again in Waco, Texas, in the fall of 1933. There, he formed a band called Bob Wills and his Playboys. A year later the band moved to KVOO radio in Tulsa, Oklahoma, where they were renamed the Texas Playboys. There, they began making musical history.

The Texas Playboys became the most famous western swing band in the country. Bob and the 13 members developed a repertoire of about 3,600 songs, moving easily from country-style jazz pieces such as "Basin Street Blues" to toe-tapping fiddle songs such as "White River Stomp," "Lone Star Rag," and others. Bob himself wrote hundreds of songs. Many were hit recordings, and one, "San Antonio Rose," was among the best sellers of all time. Bob had written it as an instrumental tune in 1938. In 1940, lyrics were added to it, and it was recorded by popular song artists such as Bing Crosby as well as by country artists. An estimated

Bob Wills (right) *poses with singer Bing Crosby, who recorded Bob's song, "San Antonio Rose."*

eight million copies were sold in the following decades.

In addition to being a noted bandleader, fiddler, and composer, Bob was an imaginative promoter with a distinctive personality. He made a deal with the Red Star Milling Company to promote its flour in exchange for a percentage of the profits from each barrel of flour sold. Later he bought his own flour mill. His flour became a nationally known brand, and the profits made him wealthy.

Bob and his band made countless personal appearances at dances. When they traveled, they rode in a bus with a big longhorn steer head on the front. Bob himself wore $100 hats and $100 boots. But even though he wore fancy clothes, he was a folk hero to his fans because of the down-to-earth way he talked to them and entertained them. He gave his uninhibited spirit free rein on stage. His familiar, drawn-out cry "Ah-h-h-h— Ha-a-a-a," often followed by, "Take it away, Leon," his lead-in to a solo by the great steel guitarist Leon McAuliffe, became a catch-phrase from coast to coast. In Dallas, he opened what some people described as the most elaborate western ballroom in the nation, with 25,000 square feet of floor space and "the longest silver dollar bar in the world."

Bob's national reputation continued to grow. He and his Texas Playboys appeared in their first movie in the early 1940s. It was a Tex Ritter film called *Take Me Back To Tulsa.* (Bob had a hit record by the same name.) More than 20 other movies followed for Bob and the Playboys throughout the 1940s and 1950s. After that, and well into the 1960s, their rhythmic, danceable music flourished on the radio, in ballrooms before capacity audiences, and in records for Columbia and other labels.

In 1968, Bob Wills was named to the Country Music Hall of Fame as "King of Western Swing... a living legend whose roadmap has charted new pathways into the world of American stage, radio, TV, records, and movies." In 1971, he was cited by the American Society of Composers, Authors and Publishers for his "long productive and creative association with country music and his unequalled leadership as a musician and man." By then, however, he had suffered the first in a series of crippling strokes that finally took his life on May 13, 1975.

The "living legend" is dead. But his music lives on through his records and in the memories of people who danced to its infectious beat in ballrooms across the nation. The unique and lively music of Bob Wills gave a new direction and "swing" to country music that is still felt today.

Patsy Montana 7

One night in 1934, Patsy Montana was sitting forlornly in her dressing room, waiting to go on stage. Her sweetheart, Paul Rose, had been away for a few days on a business trip, and she was feeling lonely. Pencil in hand, she began writing a song about how she felt.

Later Joseph L. Franks, a pioneer promoter of country music, heard the song and suggested that Patsy record it under the title "I Want To Be A Cowboy's Sweetheart." Patsy recorded the tune in 1936, and in so doing she created a milestone in the country music field. There were few women stars in country music at that time. Patsy's song was the first record by a female country singer to sell more than one million copies.

Patsy had always dreamed of becoming a western singer. Though she was drawn to western songs, her roots were actually in Arkansas. She was born on October 30, 1914, in Hot Springs, Arkansas. Her real name was Rubye Blevins.

Patsy grew up in Hot Springs and attended high school there. Then she went on to the University of Western Louisiana. All during this time, she kept practicing the guitar and learning more and more western songs. She also perfected a yodeling style that was later to earn her the nickname, the "Yodeling Cowgirl."

By the time Patsy was 20, she was already performing professionally as a western singer. To enhance her western image she took the name "Montana" from one of the songs she recorded around 1933—"When The Flowers Of Montana Are Blooming."

The next year, 1934, was an important one for Patsy. It was in 1934 that she wrote her million-seller song. It was also in that year that she married Paul Rose, the man who had inspired the song. *And* 1934 was the year during which she became lead singer for a quartet called the Prairie Ramblers. Originally, the group played old-time string band music and called themselves the "Kentucky Ramblers." But they gradually turned more and more toward the western swing music popularized by Bob Wills and others, and so they changed their name to fit the western image.

The big break for the Prairie Ramblers, and consequently for Patsy, came in 1935. They joined the featured cast of the WLS "National Barn Dance" radio broadcast from Chicago, Illinois.

Patsy on stage at Nashville West in El Monte, California, 1977

Except for the "Grand Ole Opry" in Nashville, Tennessee, the "Barn Dance" was the best known country show in the nation.

Some performers who rose to prominence on the WLS "Barn Dance," such as Gene Autry and Rex Allen, used it as a stepping stone to new phases in their careers. Patsy, however, preferred to remain with the show. She was featured for nearly 25 years, and was solo singer and star for the last 11 years of that time. She also made guest appearances throughout the country in stage shows and at county fairs, and over radio and television. She even had her own network radio program, "Wake Up And Smile," for a season on ABC.

At home among her mementos, Patsy displays a plaque awarded to her for her first hit song.

Throughout her career, Patsy continued to record cowboy and western songs for Columbia, RCA Victor, Decca, and other labels. Some of them were "I'm An Old Cowhand," "There's A Ranch In The Sky," "Singing In The Saddle," "Deep In The Heart Of Texas," and "Old Nevada Moon." She also continued to write songs such as "Me And My Cowboy Sweetheart," "My Poncho Pony," "The Buckaroo," and "Cowboy Rhythm."

Patsy tried to retire from show business in 1959. But entertaining was too much in her blood. A few years later, she started making personal appearances again. Now, some of her tours take her to foreign countries, as well as throughout the United States. In 1975 she performed in Great Britain and recorded an album there. She also gave a concert in Holland.

Today, Patsy's songs make people feel nostalgia for the old image of the West. She sings of being the "cowboy's sweetheart" who wants to "rope and ride, hear the coyotes howling, feel the wind in her face." When she describes a life "a thousand miles away from the city," listeners from all kinds of backgrounds feel a sense of freedom and escape. Nowadays, there are many successful women stars in the country music field. But the very first of them all — the first to sell a million records and one of the first to become a solo star — is the Yodeling Cowgirl, Patsy Montana.

Hank Thompson 8

In the mid-1930s, the Bob Wills brand of western swing music had begun to sweep the country, and singing cowboys had captured the fancy of the public. This was the start of a "golden age" for the western branch of country music. It came when Henry William Thompson was a boy growing up in Waco, Texas, where he had been born September 3, 1925.

The youngster was influenced by the times. His heroes were country stars such as Jimmie Rodgers, Ernest Tubb, and Gene Autry. He would wait in line to see an Autry movie, then stand to watch the movie because all the seats were taken.

Hank liked to sing western songs, and he had ability. He also showed an early talent for playing the harmonica and won several local amateur contests. But he decided that he wanted to play the guitar instead, since that was what Gene Autry played. So when Hank was 12 years old, his parents bought him a $4 guitar from a second-hand store as a Christmas present. Soon afterward, he won a prize with it at a talent show.

From then on, Hank Thompson and his guitar were seldom parted. He practiced constantly. At 17, he appeared as a guitar-picking singing cowboy on a stage show broadcast from a theater over radio WACO. A local flour company was impressed and hired him to be the host for its radio program on WACO. He was called "Hank the Hired Hand."

But World War II had begun, and six months later, Hank joined the United States Navy. He took his guitar with him. He also took his cowboy boots, but the Navy made him send those home! Hank and his guitar crossed the Pacific Ocean several times during his Navy service. He entertained his shipmates often. They enjoyed it, although Hank later joked that they either had to listen to his "pickin'" or jump overboard!

While Hank was stationed on an island in the Pacific, his ever-present guitar attracted the attention of the island people as well as that of his shipmates. An island boy once tried to trade him beads and trinkets for the instrument. Hank refused. The boy even offered to throw in the kayuk, or canoe, in which he had come. But Hank refused again. Nothing could part the singing sailor from his beloved guitar.

Thompson gained considerable musical experience during his 37 months in the Navy. He wrote songs. He sang over a chain of radio stations in the Pacific laughingly referred to as the "Mosquito Network." While stationed in California between overseas trips, he went to dances starring Bob Wills, Ernest Tubb, and others he had idolized as a boy. This was the first time Hank had ever seen these stars in person. He was fascinated by them and was amazed at how many thousands of people came to hear, and to dance to, their music.

When he was discharged from the service, he headed straight for Waco and a job with KWTX radio. He organized a band, calling it the Brazos Valley Boys, and got bookings at shows and dances in central Texas. His reputation grew. He got a better job with his original employer, WACO Radio. Then he made his first record. It was "Whoa, Sailor!", one of the songs he had written in the Navy, and it was a hit.

Tex Ritter, a cowboy movie star and one of the giants of the country music industry, heard and liked the record. He met Hank and liked him, too. Tex felt that the young man (then 21) was a potential star and helped him to get a contract with Capitol Records. Hank's first record for Capitol, "Humpty-Dumpty Heart," sold well over one million copies, and he was on his way toward fulfilling Tex Ritter's prediction.

Now, Hank has found his place among the all-time leaders in country music. He has sold more than 30 million records, including such hits as "Wild Side Of Life," "No Help Wanted," "Wake Up Irene," "Honky Tonk Girl," "A Six Pack To Go," "Smoky The Bear," and "Kindly Keep It Country." In 19 years with Capitol, and in recent years with the Dot recording label, he has had over 30 records in the country music Top 10. He has written or co-authored many hits himself, among them "Today," "Humpty-Dumpty Heart," "Honky Tonk Girl," "Yesterday's Girl," and "Rub-A-Dub-Dub."

Hank reached stardom at the end of the golden age of singing cowboys and western swing music. But he kept the music alive in a new, modern way, singing about oil wells and taverns instead of cows and sunsets. He developed his own style of western swing, with his own kind of throbbing, heavy beat. This "Thompson touch" caught on; his band, the Brazos Valley Boys, was named the number one western band by trade magazines and popularity polls for 13 consecutive years.

Like other successful western performers, Thompson has become a businessman and has found interests outside of his music career. He is an accomplished pilot with his own twin-engine airplane. With his manager, Jim Halsey, and Roy Clark, another country singer, he owns a 2,450-

acre cattle ranch outside of Tulsa, Oklahoma. He also owns a country radio station, apartment buildings, and commercial structures in the Tulsa area where he lives.

But Hank has not forgotten the importance of remaining in the public eye. He makes frequent television appearances on the "Johnny Carson Show," the "Mike Douglas Show," "Hee Haw," and other nationally known shows. He has been an annual headliner for years at the huge Texas State Fair and the Cheyenne, Wyoming, "Frontier Days" celebration. He and his band average 240 concerts on the road every year.

His fans, in turn, remain loyal. At a popular night club in Phoenix, Arizona, they swarmed over him for autographs. Some of them told him that they had first seen him perform more than 25 years earlier, and had been buying his records for at least that long. They held up old Capitol 78-rpm records for him to sign. They were letting Hank Thompson know how much they appreciated him, his music, and the fact that—in the words of one of his hit songs—he was "keeping it country."

Judy Lynn

Judy Lynn used to think that country music was "corny." The daughter of a symphony orchestra leader, she studied classical piano as a child. Later she wanted to sing popular songs and become "another Doris Day."

But the western lifestyle was also part of Judy's heritage. She was born April 12, 1936, in Boise, Idaho. Western Idaho was cowboy country, and young Judy was drawn to roping and riding horses, and competing in rodeos. She also loved to sing. As a teenager, she entertained at rodeos as both a rider and a singer, and she began to lean toward singing western songs.

Judy got her first break in country music while she was in high school. The Grand Ole Opry had come to her area as part of their tour, but their lead female performer had suddenly become ill. They needed a replacement in a hurry. The Opry people heard what a good singer Judy was and asked her to fill in with the group. She made such a hit that Opry officials took her along for the last 10 days of the tour.

Judy's good looks and talent were winning her many honors. At 16, she had been crowned Queen of the Snake River Stampede, an Idaho rodeo. In 1955, she was named Miss Idaho and went on to become runner-up in the Miss America pageant. By that time, her transition to western singer was complete. She impressed the beauty contest judges in the talent portion of the competition with her Texas-style western yodeling!

When Judy got married, her husband, John Kelly, became her manager, and the two started working on a career for Judy in country music. They lived for a year in Montana, where they had only scattered success at booking shows for her. Then they headed for Nashville, Tennessee, but were discouraged there as well.

In all, Judy spent about four years doing depressing one-night stands in small clubs for low pay. But finally the struggle began to pay off. She started appearing with Eddy Arnold, Red Foley, Rex Allen, Elvis Presley, and other "name" entertainers. The one-nighters at small clubs were gradually replaced by appearances at state fairs and college campuses, at Madison Square Garden, Carnegie Hall, and the Grand Ole Opry. Judy also put together the "Judy Lynn Show" for television, and sold it in various cities across the country. In 1962, she got a major recording contract with United Artists and, later, with Musicor and Amaret. She has turned out dozens of successful records, among them "Honey Stuff," "Footsteps Of A Fool," "My Tears Are On The Roses," and "Snowbird." Several of her hits have been her own compositions.

Through the years, Judy has been noted for her striking stage appearance. She has always worn western-style outfits. At the beginning of her career, these were homemade by her mother. After she could afford it, however, she switched to extravagant beaded outfits custom-made for her by a famous Hollywood designer named "Nudie." The rainbow-colored, heavily sequined costumes cost from $1,500 to $2,000 or more apiece, and the value of Judy's wardrobe today is estimated to be more than $75,000.

Such a high investment in an image has evidently been worthwhile. The glamorous costumes complement Judy's smooth singing, friendly stage manner, and attractive looks. And her glamorous image, in turn, has helped to make her show one of the first country and western shows to be accepted in the sophisticated hotel showrooms of Las Vegas, Nevada. The Judy Lynn Show has been featured at Caesar's Palace, the Flamingo, and other famous showrooms, where her repertoire ranges from country rock songs such as "Proud Mary," to the "Battle Hymn Of The Republic," and to the foot-stomping "Mule Skinner Blues." In one respect, however, her image-building has worked almost too well. Judy once tried to replace her elaborate western stage outfits with formal gowns. But her fans raised such a fuss that she went back to cowgirl dress!

The Las Vegas area is now the home base for the Judy Lynn Show. When she isn't on tour, Judy and her husband live at their Nevada ranch, where she spends her free time riding her show horses, tending her hives of honey bees, and enjoying the open spaces. She is happy with her life and is glad she chose a career in country music. She says that she feels about her gradual acceptance of country music the way she once felt about Southern collard greens and black-eyed peas. She didn't appreciate those either, she says, until she tried them, and then she grew to love them!

These plaques honor the achievements of Bob Wills, Tex Ritter, and Gene Autry. The plaques are on display at the Country Music Hall of Fame and Museum in Nashville, Tennessee.

Index